How to Draw Mountains, Forests and Country Landscapes!

Activity Book

PLAYBOOKS

INSTRUCTIONS FOR DRAWING:

THIS HOW-TO DRAWING BOOK CONSISTS OF IMAGES THAT ARE PLACED ON GRIDS. THERE IS AN EMPTY DRAWING BOX WITH GRIDS THAT WILL SERVE AS YOUR PRACTICE SPACE. TO COPY EACH IMAGE, DRAW PARTS OF THE IMAGE PER GRID AND PUT THEM ON THE BLANK GRIDS. SOUNDS DIFFICULT? NOT REALLY. TRY IT FIRST!

IT'S OKAY IF YOU DON'T COPY THE IMAGE PERFECTLY. AFTER ALL, DRAWING IS ABOUT THE EXPRESSION OF YOUR PERCEPTION AS WELL AS YOUR HAND STRENGTH AND CONTROL.

WHEN YOU'VE COPIED THE IMAGE, GO AHEAD AND COLOR IT NEXT! WE'RE EXCITED TO SEE WHAT YOU CAN DO!

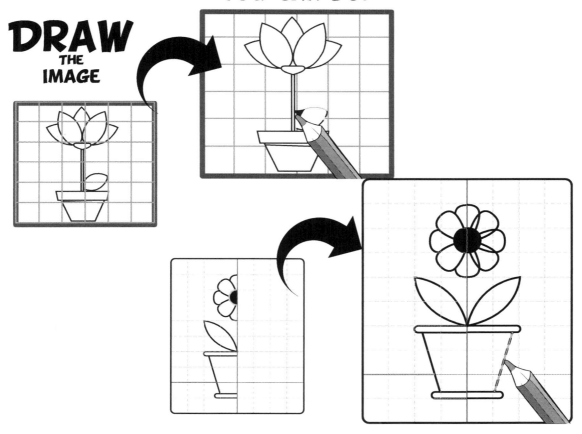

DRAW THE IMAGE

DRAW
THE
IMAGE

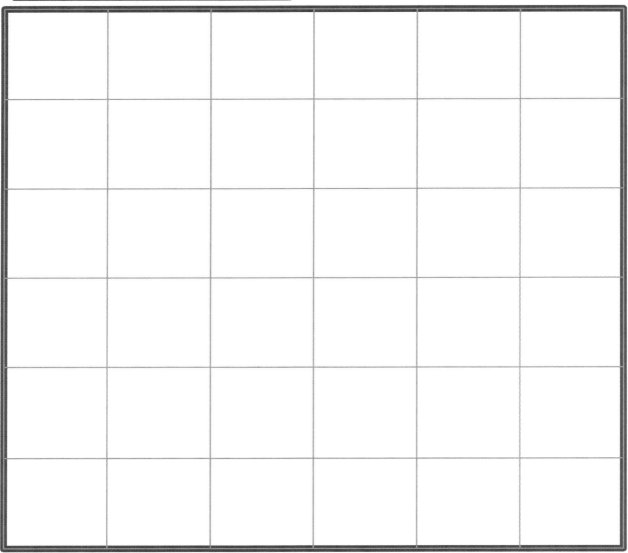

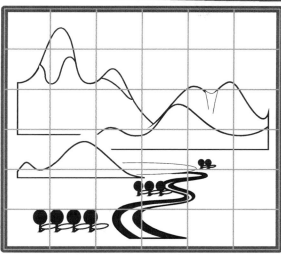

DRAW
THE
IMAGE

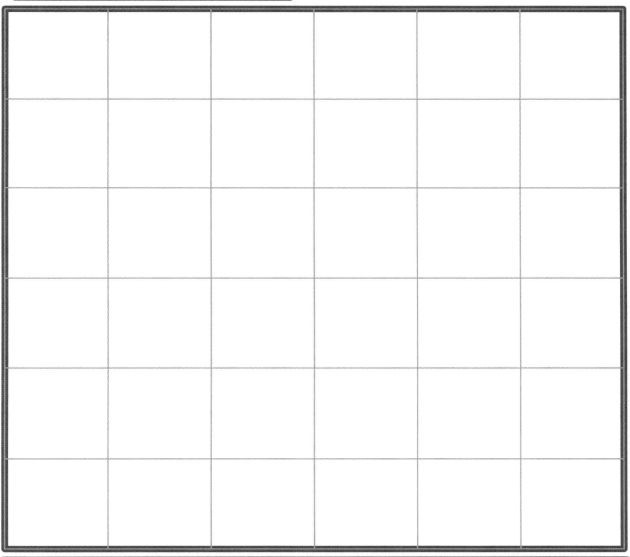

DRAW
THE
IMAGE

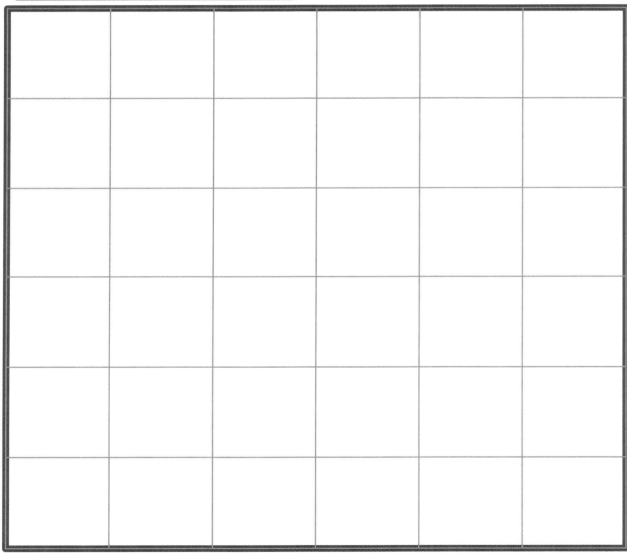

DRAW
THE
IMAGE

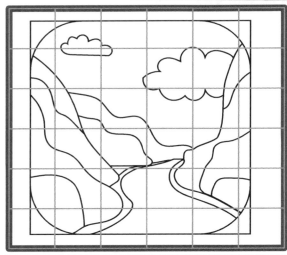

DRAW
THE
IMAGE

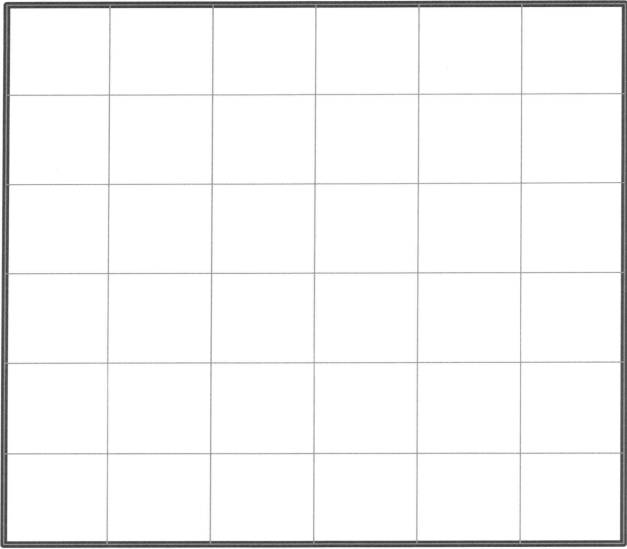

DRAW
THE
IMAGE

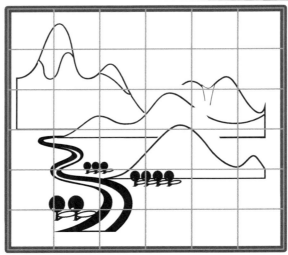

DRAW
THE
IMAGE

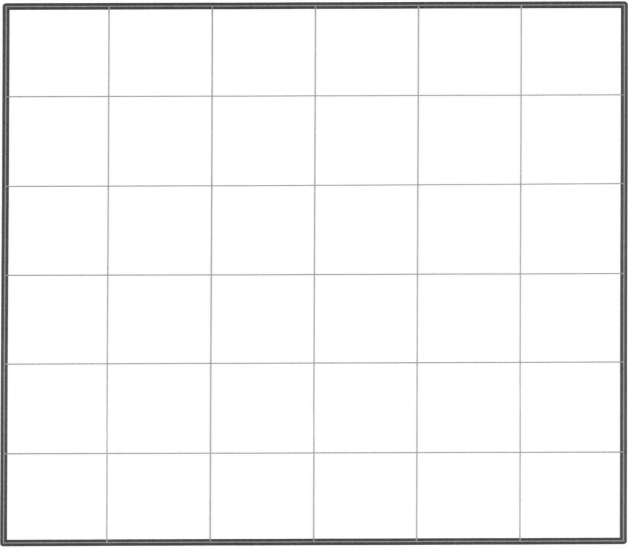

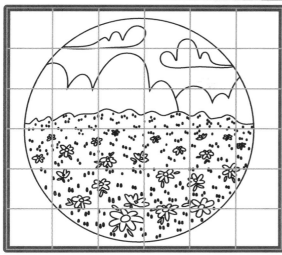

DRAW
THE
IMAGE

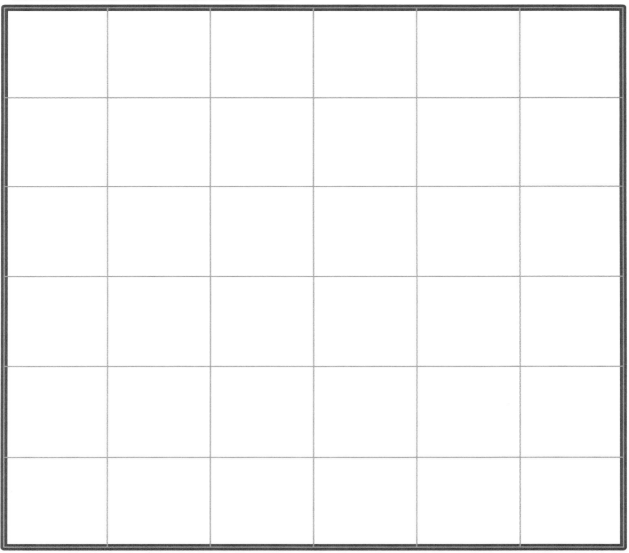

DRAW
THE
IMAGE

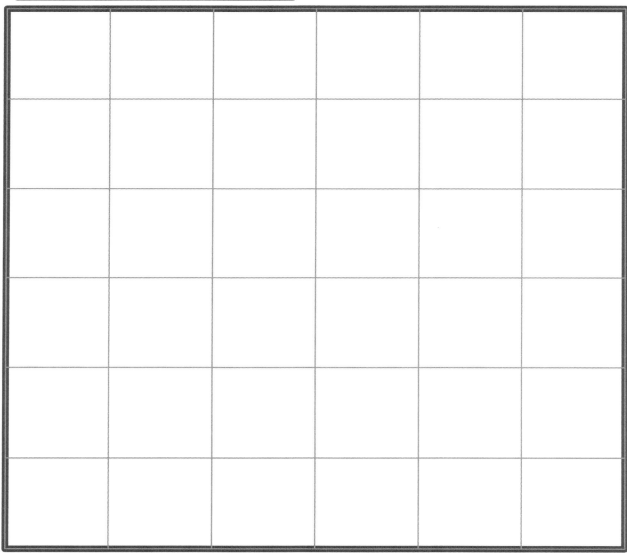

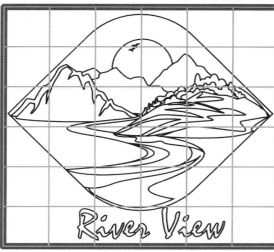

River View

DRAW
THE
IMAGE

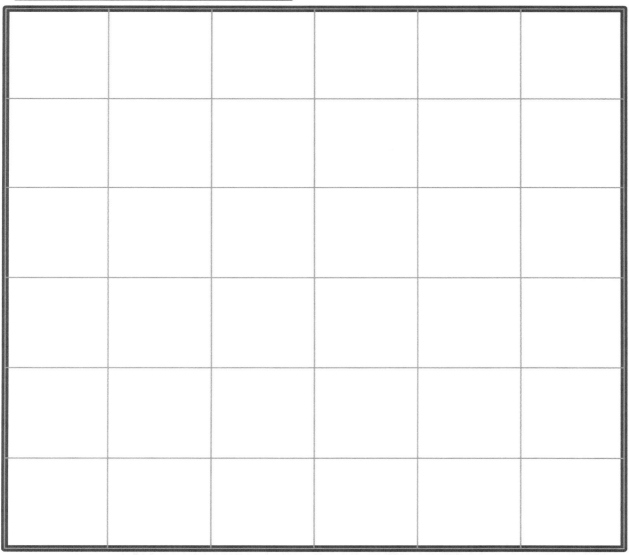

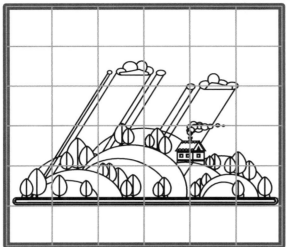

DRAW
THE
IMAGE

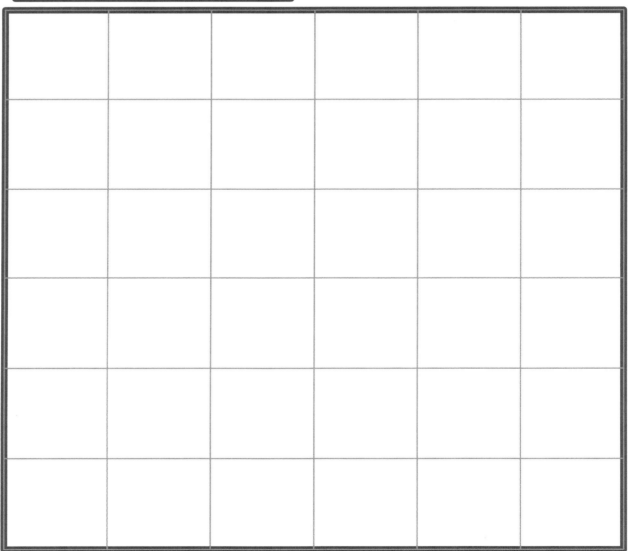

DRAW
THE
IMAGE

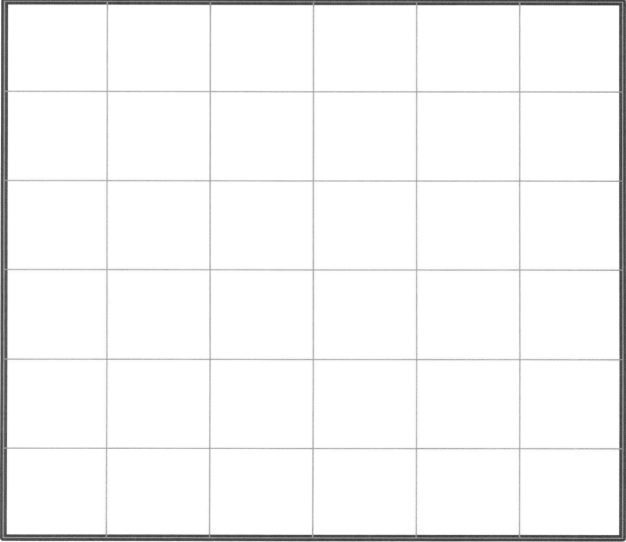

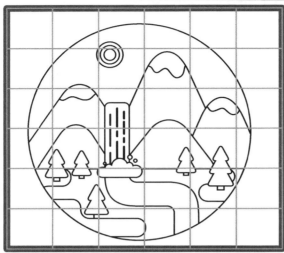

DRAW
THE
IMAGE

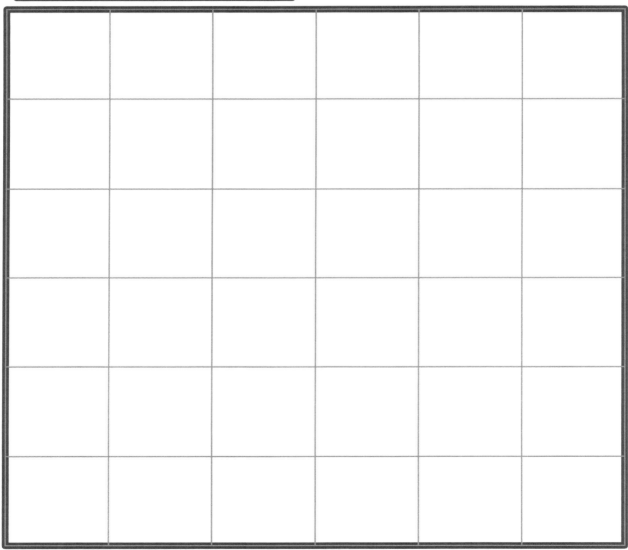

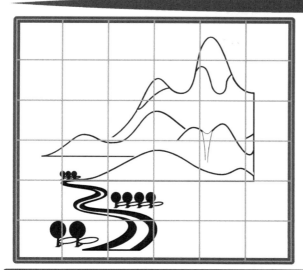

DRAW
THE
IMAGE

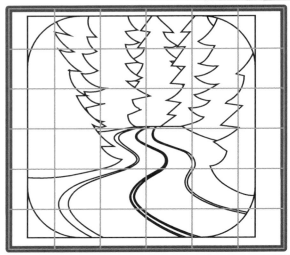

DRAW
THE
IMAGE

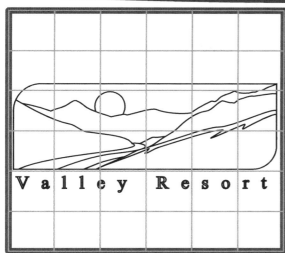

Valley Resort

DRAW
THE
IMAGE

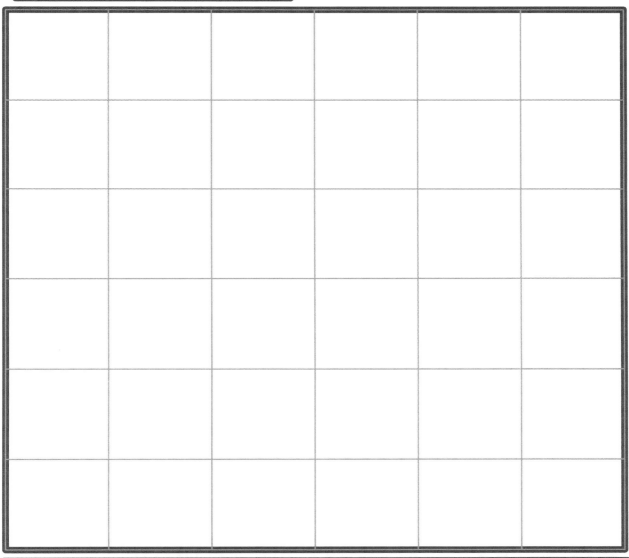

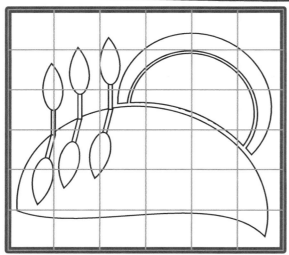

DRAW
THE
IMAGE

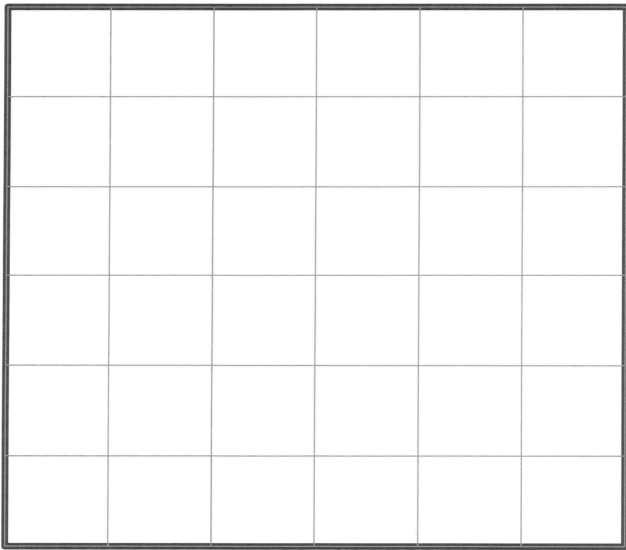

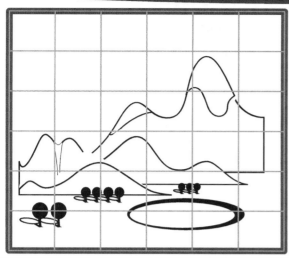

DRAW
THE
IMAGE

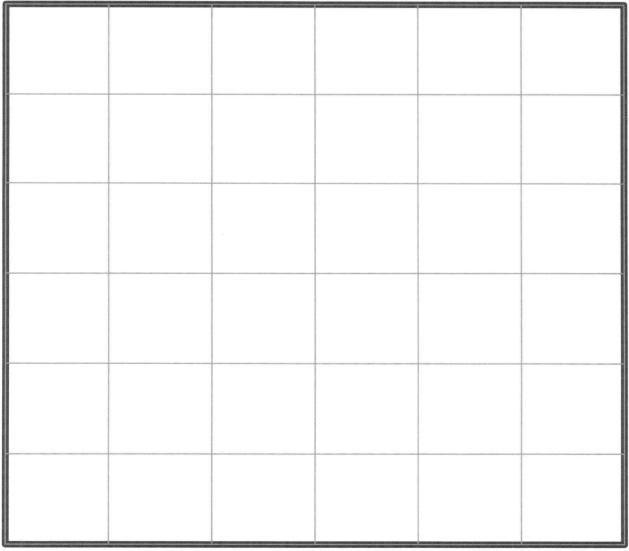

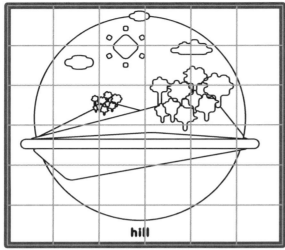

hill

DRAW
THE
IMAGE

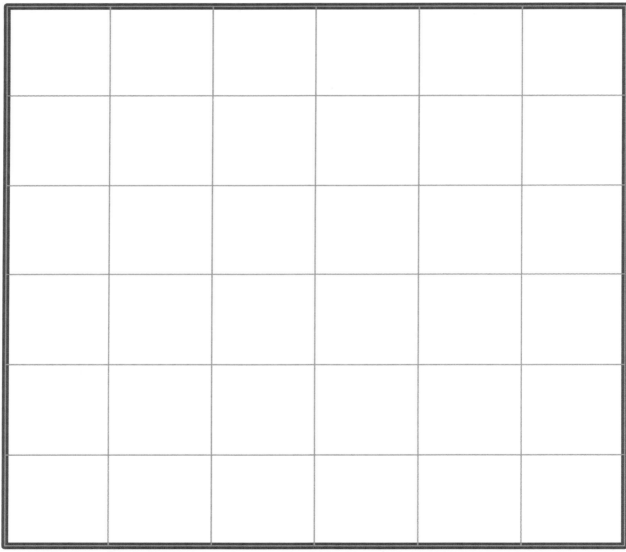

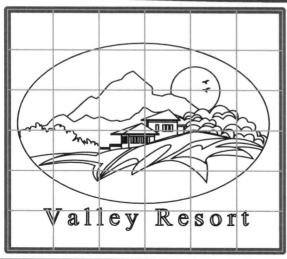

Valley Resort

DRAW
THE
IMAGE

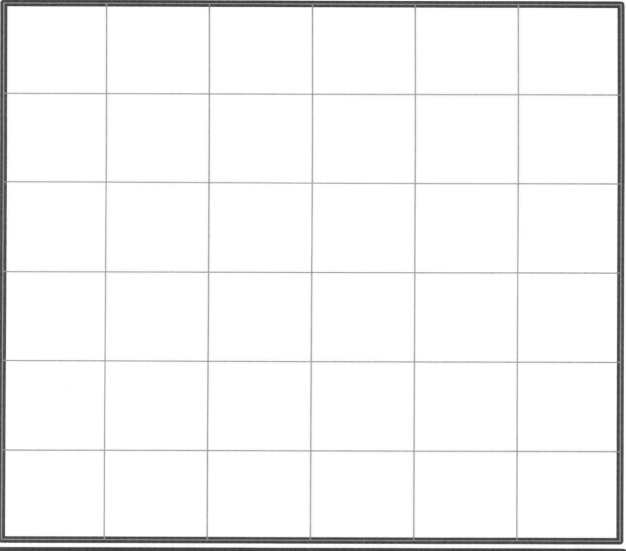

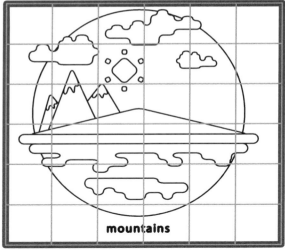

mountains

DRAW
THE
IMAGE

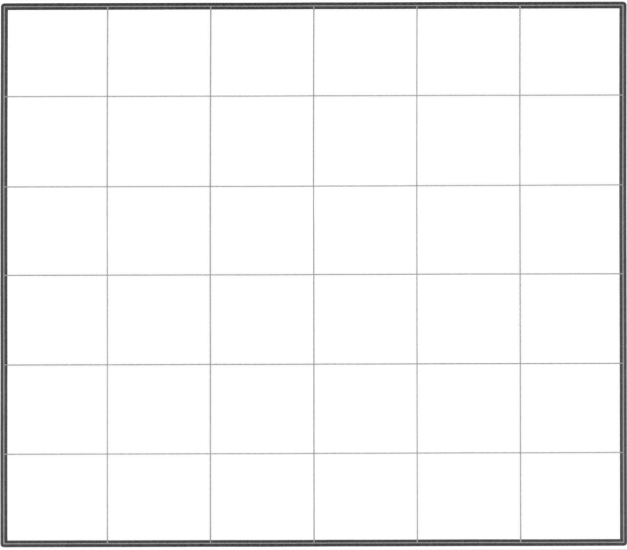

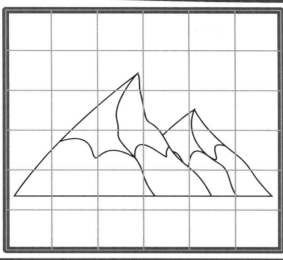

DRAW
THE
IMAGE

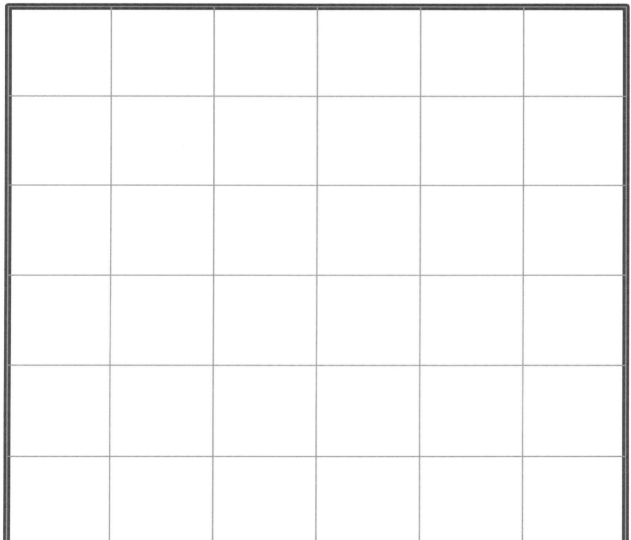

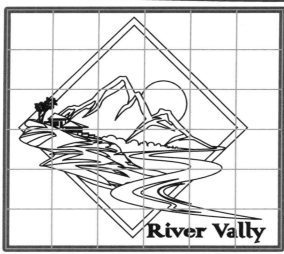

River Vally

DRAW
THE
IMAGE

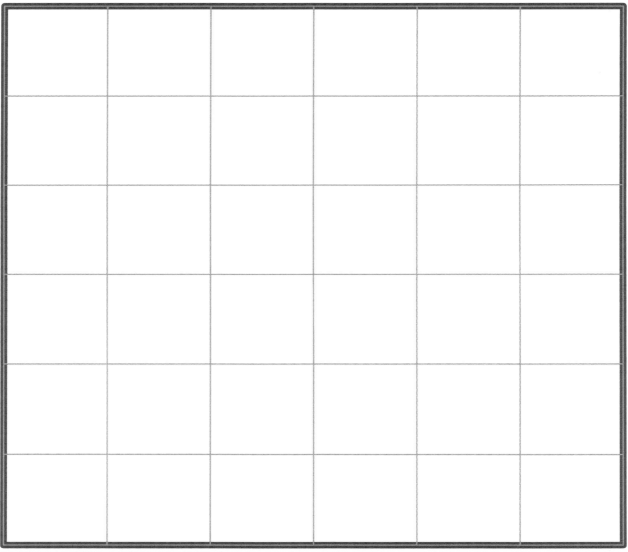

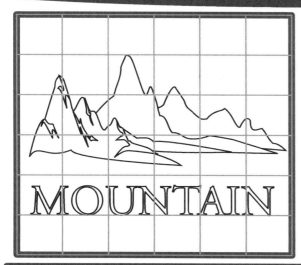

MOUNTAIN

DRAW
THE
IMAGE

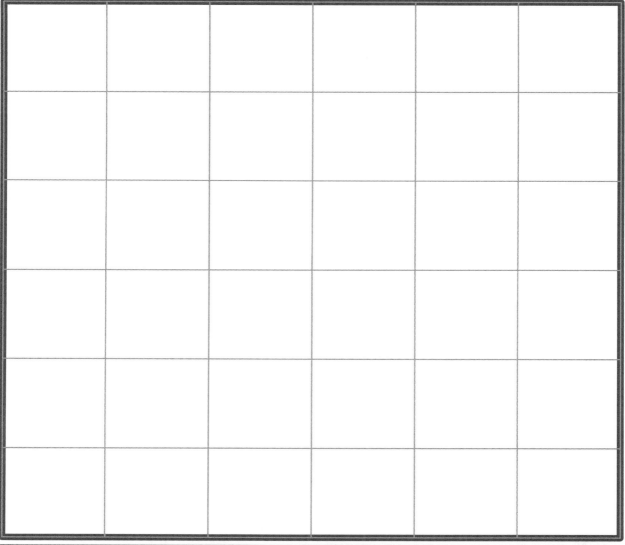

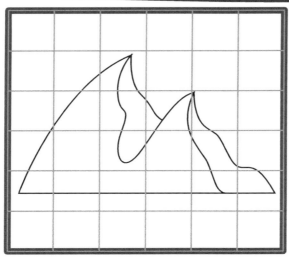

DRAW
THE
IMAGE

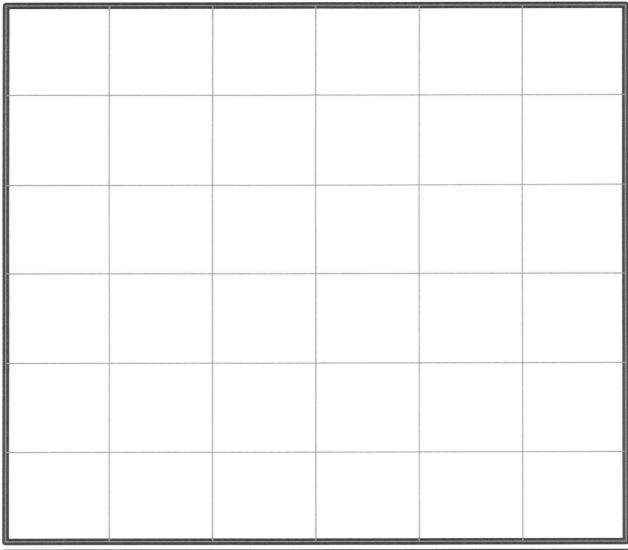

DRAW
THE
IMAGE

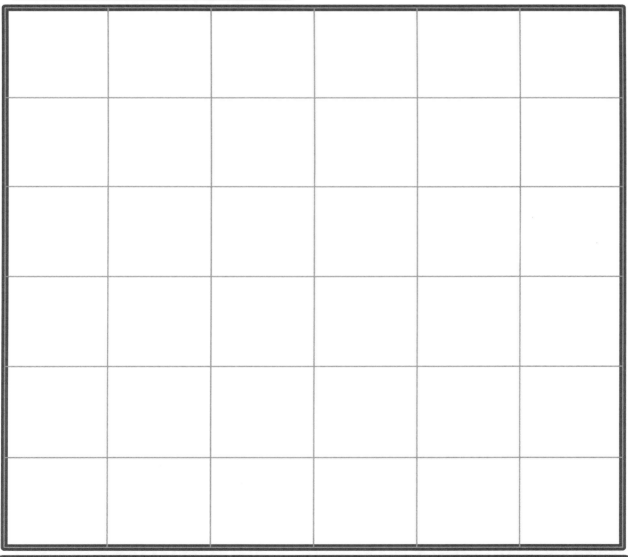

DRAW
THE
IMAGE

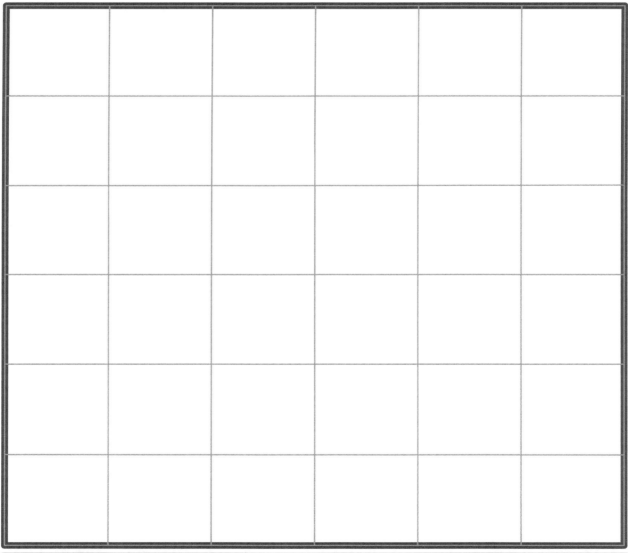

DRAW
THE
IMAGE

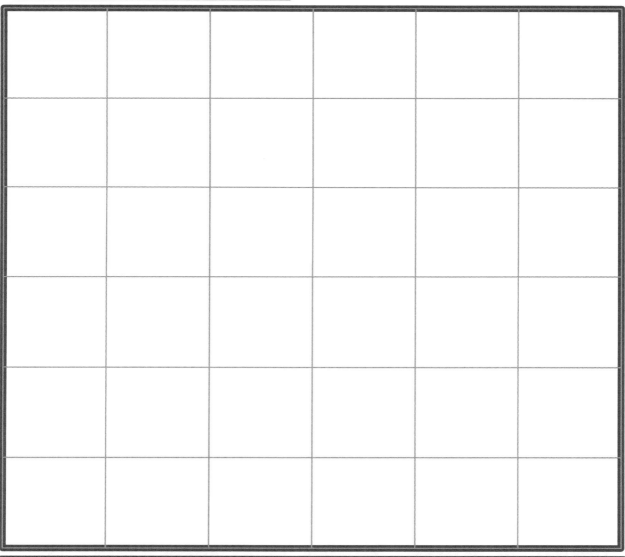

DRAW
THE
IMAGE

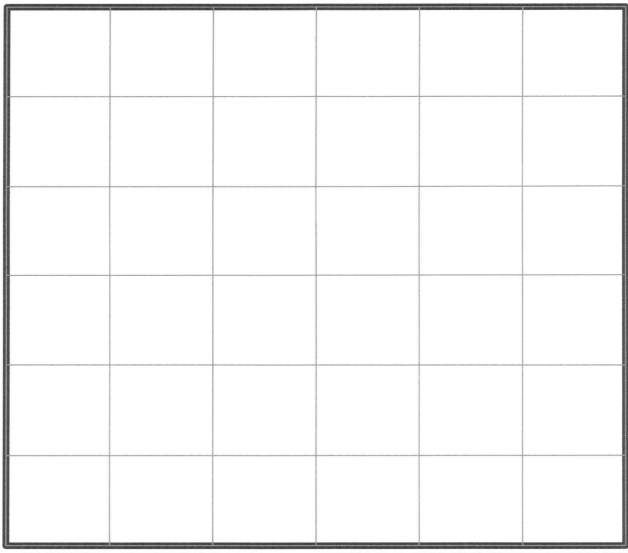

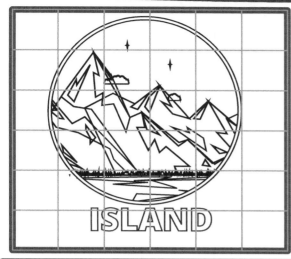

ISLAND

DRAW
THE
IMAGE

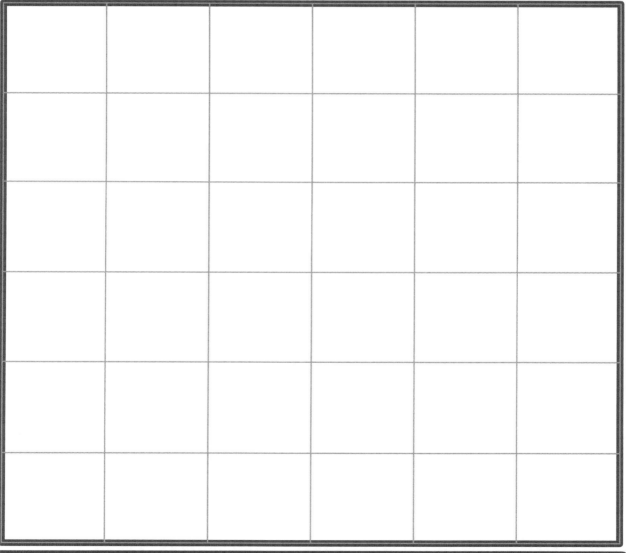

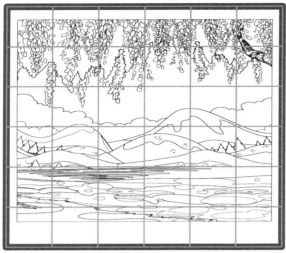

DRAW
THE
IMAGE

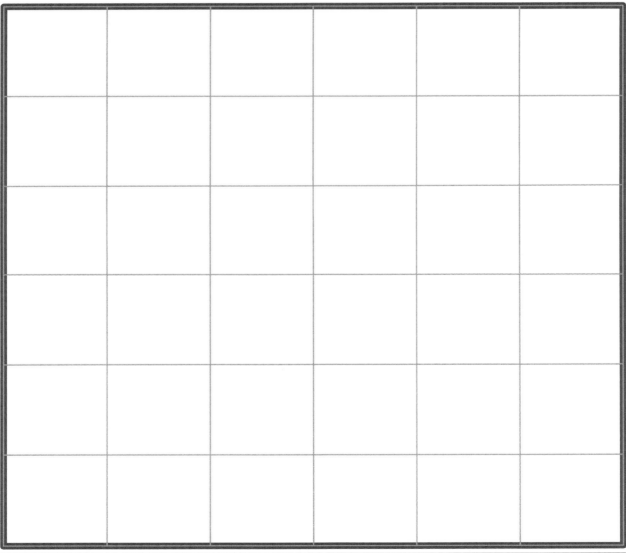

DRAW
THE
IMAGE

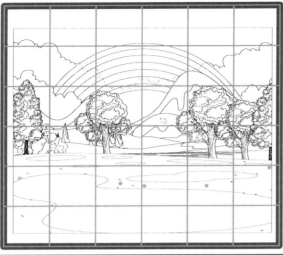

DRAW
THE
IMAGE

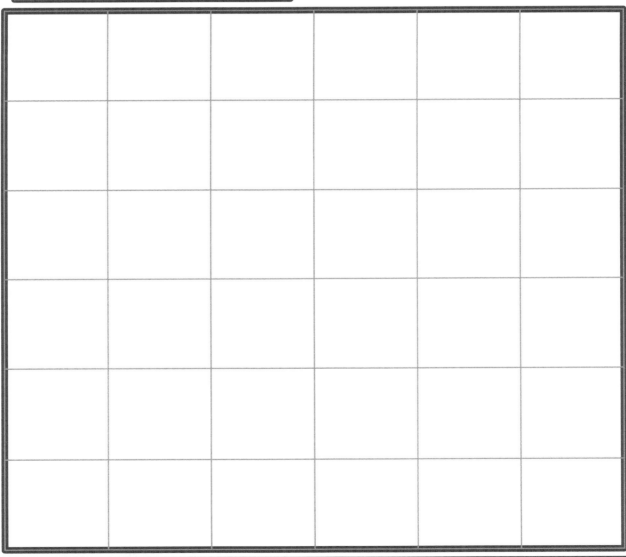

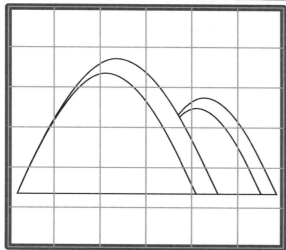

DRAW
THE
IMAGE

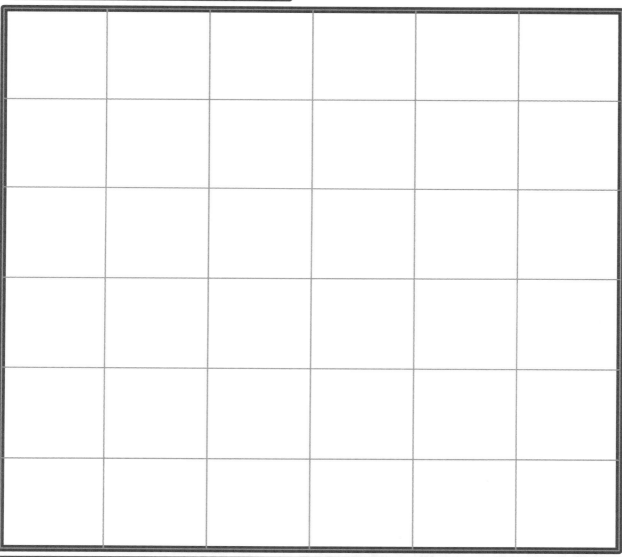

DRAW
THE
IMAGE

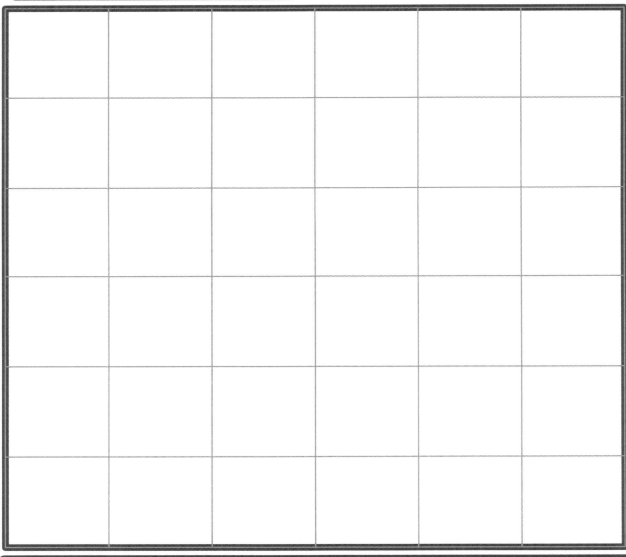

DRAW
THE
IMAGE

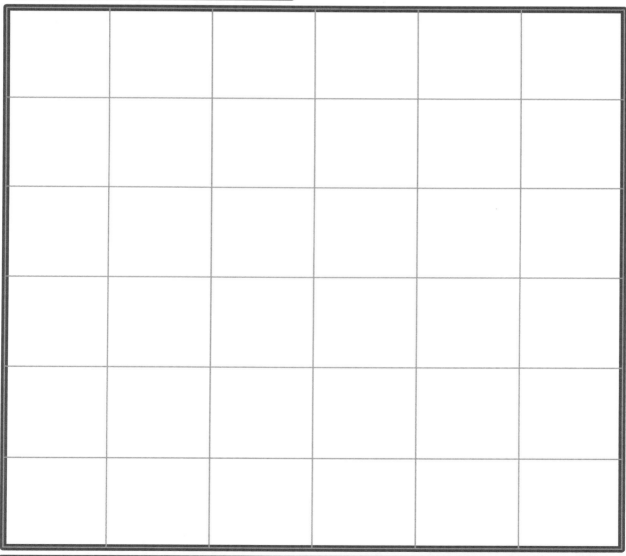

Made in the USA
Las Vegas, NV
22 December 2020